Baby Animals in Action!

BW
BOOKWORMS

Kittens

By Nicole Horning

Cavendish Square
New York

Published in 2021 by Cavendish Square Publishing, LLC
243 5th Avenue, Suite 136, New York, NY 10016

First Edition

Library of Congress Cataloging-in-Publication Data

Names: Horning, Nicole, author.
Title: Kittens / Nicole Horning.
Description: First edition. | New York : Cavendish Square Publishing, [2021] |
Series: Baby animals in action! | Includes index.
Identifiers: LCCN 2019059381 (print) | LCCN 2019059382 (ebook) |
ISBN 9781502656155 (library binding) | ISBN 9781502656131 (paperback) |
ISBN 9781502656148 (set) | ISBN 9781502656162 (ebook)
Subjects: LCSH: Kittens–Juvenile literature.
Classification: LCC SF447 .H66 2021 (print) | LCC SF447 (ebook) |
DDC 636.8/07–dc23
LC record available at https://lccn.loc.gov/2019059381
LC ebook record available at https://lccn.loc.gov/2019059382

Editor: Nicole Horning
Copy Editor: Nathan Heidelberger
Designer: Deanna Paternostro

The photographs in this book are used by permission and through the courtesy of: Cover CebotariN/Shutterstock.com; p. 5 Esin Deniz/Shutterstock.com; p. 7 Nastivan/Shutterstock.com; p. 9 Lipatova Maryna/Shutterstock.com; p. 11 Andrey Khusnutdinov/Shutterstock.com; p. 13 Anca Popa/Shutterstock.com; p. 15 ANURAK PONGPATIMET/Shutterstock.com; p. 17 wavebreakmedia/Shutterstock.com; p. 19 Vagengeim/Shutterstock.com; p. 21 Elizaveta Galitckaia/Shutterstock.com; p. 23 Chendongshan/Shutterstock.com.

Printed in the United States of America

CONTENTS

How Kittens Grow

Cats often make great pets for people. Kittens are baby cats. Kittens that go to live with people stay with their mother for around 12 weeks first. Then, they're ready to join a new family.

Kittens are part of a **litter** when they're born. The mother cat feeds them milk. Kittens can't open their eyes or ears until they're around one week old. They start walking at around three weeks old.

When kittens open their eyes, they can see in the dark better than people can! This is one way kittens have **adapted** over many years. However, they have trouble seeing colors or objects that are far away.

Kittens' claws stay covered in their paws most of the time. Kittens can also make their claws stick out. Their claws can come out when they're **scratching**, playing, or catching something.

Kitten Lives

Kittens drink milk until they're around one month old. Next, they start eating wet kitten food. Over time, the wet food can be made drier. It takes a long time before kittens can start eating dry food.

Kittens sleep for most of the day. They sleep 18 to 22 hours a day! When they get older, they sleep 12 to 16 hours a day. Because of how they've adapted, they're awake most of the night.

Kittens need to be taken to the **veterinarian** a lot when they're young. This is to make sure they stay healthy as they grow up. When they get older, they can go less often.

Kittens and People

Kittens use sounds to let people know what they're feeling. They may meow when they want food or water. They hiss when they want to be left alone. Cats often purr when they're happy. If their ears are back and they're purring, they're worried.

Kittens may get scared when meeting a new person. If you're meeting your new kitten or your friend's kitten for the first time, it's important to say hello the right way. First, kneel down if the kitten is on the floor.

Next, reach out your hand for the kitten to smell. If it rubs its head on your hand, you can slowly pet it. It may even let you play with it using a ball or toy mouse!

WORDS TO KNOW

adapted: Changed in order to live better in a certain place.

litter: A group of baby animals born to a mother animal all at one time.

scratching: Digging with the claws.

veterinarian: A doctor who takes care of animals.

INDEX